THE BOOK OF GOOD CHEER

D1040944

THE BOOK OF GOOD CHEER

EDITED BY EDWIN GROVER

LAUGHING ELEPHANT BOOKS SEATTLE 2000

THE BOOK OF GOOD CHEER

A reprint of a book originally published
by P.F. Volland and Company in 1913.

Copyright © 2000   Blue Lantern Studio
All rights reserved.   First printing.   Printed in Singapore.

ISBN 1-883211-27-1

Laughing Elephant Books
Post Office Box 4399   Seattle Washington   98104

*G*OOD CHEER is contagious. It is an outward expression of an inward faith that

"God's in his Heaven,
All's right with the world!"

The man who radiates good cheer, who makes life happier wherever he meets it, is always a man of vision and of faith. He sees the blossoming flower in the tiny seed, the silver lining to every cloud, and a beautiful tomorrow in the darkest today.

Good cheer is something more than faith in the future, it is gratitude for the past and joy in the present. Life for all of us has its hardships and disappointments. It is out of such stuff as this that human character is made. But after all, this world is a pretty good place and we at least owe each other the courtesy of a smiling face and the inspiration of a cheery word.

To go about our work with pleasure, to greet others with a word of encouragement, to be happy in the present and confident of the future, this is to have achieved some measure of success in living.

This "Little Bundle of Cheery Thoughts" has been gathered through long years of joyous search for the right word fitly spoken. They come from some of the wisest men of all time and ought to be perpetual inspiration to us all.

THE GOSPEL OF GOOD CHEER

IN the laughter of the little brook
That runs its merry way,
From the mountain-sides of Yesterday
To the meadows of Today;

In the song of every happy bird,
In the bloom of every flower,
In the blue, blue sky above us,
And the sun behind the shower;

In the laughter of the children,
In the faces that they bear,—
Behold the joyous tidings,
And the glory everywhere!

There's a smile wher'er we journey,
There's a laugh we all may hear,
If we'll only hark and listen
To the Gospel of Good Cheer.

—Edwin Osgood Grover

TWIXT optimist and pessimist the difference is droll;
The optimist sees the doughnut, the pessimist the hole.

CLOUDS may come, but clouds must go,
And they have a silver lining.
For beyond them all, you know,
Either sun or moon is shining.
So with trouble; 'tis quite plain
Time at last will take its measure;
Rainbows follow after rain,
Life must have its meed of pleasure.

—J. A. W.

GOD bless the heart of sunshine
That smiles the clouds away,
And sets a star of fresh-born hope
In some one's sky each day.
God bless all words of kindness
That lift the heart from gloom,
And in life's barren places
Plant flowers of love to bloom.

—A. H. G.

IT IS no use to grumble and complain;
It's just as cheap and easy to rejoice,
When God sorts out the weather and sends rain—
Why, rain's my choice.

—James Whitcomb Riley

SUNSHINE

SOMEWHERE on the great world the sun is always shining and just so sure as you live, it will sometime shine on you. The dear God has made it so. There is so much sunshine we must all have our share.

—Myrtle Reed

LIKE the star
Which shines afar,
Without haste,
Without rest,
Let each one wheel
With steady stay
Round the task
Which rules the day
And do his best.

I AM bigger than anything that can happen to me. All these things, sorrow, misfortune and suffering, are outside my door. I am in the house and I have the key.

—Charles F. Lummis

EAT less; breathe more.
Talk less; think more.
Ride less; walk more.
Clothe less; bathe more.
Worry less; work more.
Waste less; give more.
Preach less; practice more.

TODAY

THINK not on yesterday, nor trouble borrow
On what may be in store for you Tomorrow,
But let Today be your incessant care,—
The past is past, Tomorrow's in the air.
Who gives Today the best that in him lies
Will find the road that leads to clearer skies.

—John Kendrick Bangs

IT is not raining rain to me,
    It's raining daffodils,
In every dimpled drop I see
    Wild flowers on the hills.

The clouds of gray engulf the day
    And overwhelm the town;
It is not raining rain to me,
    It's raining roses down.

It is not raining rain to me,
    But fields of clover bloom,
Where any buccaneering bee
    Can find a bed and room.

A health unto the happy,
    A fig for him who frets!
It is not raining rain to me,
    It's raining violets!

—Robert Loveman

THE TASK OF HAPPINESS

IF I have faltered more or less
In my great task of happiness;
If I have moved among my race
And shown no glorious morning face;
If beams from happy human eyes
Have moved me not; if morning skies,
Books, and my food, and summer rain
Knocked on my sullen heart in vain:—
Lord, Thy most pointed pleasure take
And stab my spirit broad awake;
Or, Lord, if too obdurate I,
Choose Thou, before that spirit die,
A piercing pain, a killing sin,
And to my dead heart run them in!

—Robert Louis Stevenson

I WOULD rather be able to appreciate things I cannot have, than to have things I am not able to appreciate.

THE wealth of a man is the number of things he loves and blesses, which he is loved and blessed by.

—Thomas Carlyle

TO give pleasure to a single heart by a single kind act is better than a thousand head-bowings in prayer.

—Saadi

WHEN the outlook is not good, try the uplook.

WE just shake hands at meeting
    With many that come nigh;
We nod the head in greeting
    To many that go by—

But welcome through the gateway
    Our few old friends and true;
Then hearts leap up, and straightway
    There's open house for you,
      Old friends,
    There's open house for you!

—Gerald Massey

MY BUSINESS is not to remake myself,
But to make the absolute best of what God made.

—Robert Browning

DO not keep the alabaster box of your love and tenderness sealed up until your friends are dead. Fill their lives with sweetness. Speak approving, cheering words while their ears can hear them, and while their hearts can be thrilled and made happier. The kind things you mean to say when they are gone, say before they go. The flowers you mean to send for their coffin, send to brighten and sweeten their homes before they leave them.

Let us learn to anoint our friends while they are yet among the living. Post-mortem kindness does not cheer the burdened heart; flowers on the coffin cast no fragrance backward over the weary way.

—George W. Childs

GOD help me speak the little word
And take my bit of singing.

I FIND earth not gray but rosy,
    Heaven not grim but fair of hue.
Do I stoop? I pluck a posy.
    Do I stand and stare? All's blue.

—Robert Browning

THE HUMAN TOUCH

HIGH thoughts and noble in all lands
    Help me; my soul is fed by such.
But ah, the touch of lips and hands,—
    The human touch!
Warm, vital, close, life's symbols dear,—
These need I most, and now, and here.

—Richard Burton

IF THAT WERE ENOUGH

TO thrill with the joy of girded men,
To go on forever and fail and go on again,
To be mauled to the earth and arise,
And contend for the shade of a word and
        a thing not seen with the eyes:
With the half of a broken hope for a pillow at night,
That somehow the right is the right
And the smooth shall bloom from the rough:
Lord, if that were enough!

—Robert Louis Stevenson

ONE who claims that he knows about it
    Tells me the earth is a vale of sin;
But I and the bees, and the birds, we doubt it,
    And think it a world worth living in.
                —Ella Wheeler Wilcox

THE inner side of every cloud is bright and shining;
    I therefore turn my clouds about
    And always wear them inside out
To show the lining.
               —Ellen Thorncroft Fowler

IT'S the song ye sing, and the smiles ye wear,
That's a-makin' the sun shine everywhere.
               —James Whitcomb Riley

IF the world is going wrong,
    Forget it!
Sorrow never lingers long—
    Forget it!
If your neighbor bears ill-will,
If your conscience won't be still,
If you owe an ancient bill!
    Forget it!

THE soul would have no rainbow
Had the eyes no tears.
               —John Vance Cheney

SPIN cheerfully,
Not tearfully,
  Though wearily you plod.
Spin carefully,
Spin prayerfully,
  But leave the thread with God.

WHAT we call Luck
  Is simply Pluck,
  And doing things over and over;
  Courage and will,
  Perseverance and skill,—
Are the four leaves of Luck's clover.

THE GIST OF LIFE

TO be up and doing, O
Unfearing and unshamed to go
In all the uproar and the press
About my human business!
My undissuaded heart I hear
Whisper courage in my ear.
With voiceless calls, the ancient earth
Summons me to a daily birth.
Thou, O my love, ye, O my friends—
The gist of life, the end of ends—
To laugh, to love, to live, to die,
Ye call me by the ear and eye!

                              —Robert Louis Stevenson

OUR KIND OF A MAN

THE kind of a man for you and me!
He faces the world unflinchingly,
And smiles as long as the wrong exists,
With a knuckled faith and force like fists:
He lives the life he is preaching of,
And loves where most is the need of love;
And feeling still, with a grief half glad,
That the bad are as good as the good are bad,
He strikes straight out for the right—and he
Is the kind of a man for you and me!

—James Whitcomb Riley

IF YOU have knowledge, let others light their candles by it.

—Thomas Fuller

THE people who always live in houses, and sleep on beds, and walk on pavements, and buy their food from butchers and bakers and grocers, are not the most blessed inhabitants of this wide and various earth. The circumstances of their existence are too mathematical and secure for perfect contentment. They live at second or third hand. They are boarders in the world. Everything is done for them by somebody else.

—Henry van Dyke

IN THE school of life many branches of knowledge are taught. But the only philosophy that amounts to anything after all, is just the secret of making friends with our luck.

—Henry van Dyke

THE SONG ON THE WAY

ANY way the old world goes
    Happy be the weather!
With the red thorn or the rose
    Singin' all together!
Don't you see that sky o' blue!
    Good Lord painted it for you!
Reap the daisies in the dew
    Singin' all together!
Springtime sweet, an' frosty fall
    Happy be the weather!
Earth has gardens for us all,
    Goin' on together.
Sweet the labor in the light,
    To the harvest's gold and white—
Till the toilers say "Good night,"
    Singin' all together!

THREE KINDS OF COURAGE

THERE'S the courage that nerves you in starting to climb
    The mount of success rising sheer;
And when you've slipped back there's the courage sublime
    That keeps you from shedding a tear.

These two kinds of courage, I give you my word,
    Are worthy of tribute—but then,
You'll not reach the summit unless you've the third—
    The courage of try-it-again!

—Roy Farrell Greene

IMAGINATION is the supreme gift of the gods, and the degree of its possession is the measure of any man's advantage over circumstance—the measure of his clutch on Success.

—James Howard Kehler

GOD be thanked, whate'er comes after, I have lived and toiled with men.

—Rudyard Kipling

TO know what you prefer, instead of humbly saying "Amen," to what the world tells you you ought to prefer, is to have kept your soul alive.

—Robert Louis Stevenson

OF what shall a man be proud if he is not proud of his friends?

—Robert Louis Stevenson

NO medieval mystery, no crowned,
   Dim figure, halo ringed, uncanny bright;
A modern saint: a man who treads earth's ground,
   And ministers to men with all his might!

—Richard Burton

DO not worry; eat three square meals a day; say your prayers; be courteous to your creditors; keep your digestion good; exercise; go slow, and easy. Maybe there are other things that your special case requires to make you happy, but, my friend, these I reckon will give you a good life.

—Abraham Lincoln

SUN PHILOSOPHY

*S*MILE!
This advice is worth a pile—
Beats ter blazes strikin' ile;
When yer blood begins ter bile,
Jes' you smile!

Smile!
Let the other feller cuss;
'Taint your biz ter make a fuss;
You can clear away the muss
With a smile.

Smile!
When things go tarnation wrong
Buck your courage with a song;
Luck can't lose you very long
Ef you smile.

Smile!
'Til the bluey heavens shine thro',
An, ole Sol winks down at you;
Thinks you are a sunbeam too,
'Cause you smile.

—Florence M. Pierce

I'LL not confer with sorrow
Till tomorrow;
But joy shall have her way
This very day.

—T. B. Aldrich

THE WORD

TODAY, whatever may annoy,
The word for me is Joy, just simple joy:
The joy of life;
The joy of children and of wife;
The joy of bright, blue skies;
The joy of rain; the glad surprise
Of twinkling stars that shine at night;
The joy of winged things upon their flight;
The joy of noon-day, and the tried
True joyousness of eventide;
The joy of labor, and of mirth;
The joy of air, and sea, and earth —
The countless joys that ever flow from Him
Whose vast beneficence doth dim
The lustrous light of day,
And lavish gifts divine upon our way.
    Whate'er there be of Sorrow
     I'll put off till Tomorrow,
And when Tomorrow comes, why then
'Twill be Today and Joy again!

—John Kendrick Bangs

WHY thus longing, thus forever sighing,
    For the far off, unattained and dim?
While the beautiful, all around thee lying,
    Offers its low, perpetual hymn.

—Harriet Winslow

SO many gods, so many creeds,
    So many paths that wind and wind;
When just the art of being kind
    Is all the sad world needs.

            —Ella Wheeler Wilcox

FORGET thyself and all thy woes,
    Put out each feverish light;
The stars are watching overhead;
    Sleep sweet. Good night! Good night!

DON'T do anything, till you do it; and when you've done it, stop doing it.

            —William Gillette

TO be honest, to be kind—to earn a little and to spend a little less, to make upon the whole a family happier for his presence; to renounce when that shall be necessary and not to be embittered; to keep a few friends, but these without capitulation—above all, on the same grim conditions, to keep friends with himself—here is a task for all that a man has of fortitude and delicacy.

            —Robert Louis Stevenson

 I WISH, I can, I will—these are the three trumpet notes to victory.

DO NOT hurry,
Do not worry,
As this world you travel through,
No regretting,
Fuming, fretting,
Ever can advantage you.
Be content with what you've done;
What on earth you leave undone,
There are plenty left to do.

—P. M. Wyline

THERE is an idea abroad among moral people that they should make their neighbors good. One person I have to make good: myself. But my duty to my neighbor is much more nearly expressed by saying that I have to make him happy—if I may.

—Robert Louis Stevenson

I AM happy in having learned to distinguish between ownership and possession. Books, pictures, and all the beauty of the world belong to those who love and understand them—not usually to those who possess them. All of these things that I am entitled to, I have—I own them by divine right. So, I care not a bit who possesses them. I used to care very much and consequently was very unhappy.

—James Howard Kehler

NOW

IF YOU have hard work to do,
    Do it now.
Today the skies are clear and blue,
Tomorrow clouds may come in view,
Yesterday is not for you;
    Do it now.
If you have a song to sing,
    Sing it now.
Let the tones of gladness ring
Clear as song of bird in spring.
Let every day some music bring;
    Sing it now.
If you have kind words to say,
    Say them now.
Tomorrow may not come your way,
Do a kindness while you may;
Loved ones will not always stay;
    Say them now.
If you have a smile to show,
    Show it now.
Make hearts happy, roses grow,
Let the friends around you know
The love you have before they go;
    Show it now.

DAYS change so many things—yes, hours—
We see so differently in suns and showers.

—George Klingle

HE common problem, yours, mine, everyone's
Is—not to fancy what were fair in life
Provided it could be; but finding first
What may be, then find how to make it fair
Up to our means, a very different thing!

—Robert Browning

BE STRONG

E strong!
We are not here to play, to dream to drift;
We have hard work to do, and loads to lift;
Shun not the struggle—face it; 'tis God's gift.

Be strong!
Say not, "The days are evil. Who's to blame?"
And fold the hands and acquiesce—oh shame!
Stand up, speak out, and bravely, in God's name.

Be strong!
It matters not how deep intrenched the wrong,
How hard the battle goes, the day how long;
Faint not—fight on! Tomorrow comes the song.

—Maltbie Davenport Babcock

HERE is no duty we so much underrate as the duty of being happy. By being happy we sow anonymous benefits upon the world, which remain unknown even to ourselves, or when they are disclosed, surprise nobody so much as the benefactor.

—Robert Louis Stevenson

WHEN THE BIRDS GO NORTH AGAIN

OH, EVERY year hath its winter,
    And every year hath its rain—
But a day is always coming
    When the birds go north again.

When new leaves swell in the forest,
    And grass springs green on the plain,
And the alders' veins turn crimson—
    And the birds go north again.

Oh, every heart hath its sorrow,
    And every heart hath its pain—
But a day is always coming
    When the birds go north again.

'Tis the sweetest thing to remember
    If courage be on the wane,
When the cold, dark days are over—
    Why, the birds go north again.

—Ella Higginson

TO BE what we are, and to become what we are capable of becoming, is the only end of life.

—Robert Louis Stevenson

TO BE polite is to do and say
    The kindest things in the kindest way.

—Sophia Bronson Titterington

DON'T GIT SORRY FER YERSELF

DON'T you go and git sorry fer yerself. That's one thing I can't stand in nobody. There's always lots of other folks you kin be sorry fer 'sted of yerself. Ain't you proud you ain't got a hairlip? Why, that one thought is enough to keep me from *ever* gittin' sorry fer myself.

—Mrs. Wiggs

I WOULD not give a farthing for a man's religion if his dog and cat are not the better for it.

—Rowland Hill

THERE has not been a single day since the world began when the sun was not shining. The trouble has been with our vision.

GENTLENESS and cheerfulness, these come before all morality; they are the perfect duties. If your morals make you dreary, depend upon it they are wrong. I do not say "give them up," for they may be all you have; but conceal them like a vice, lest they should spoil the lives of better and simpler people.

—Robert Louis Stevenson

BUT in the mud and scum of things
There always, always, something sings.

—Ralph Waldo Emerson

LOOKS like ever'thing in the world comes right if we jes' wait long enough.

—Mrs. Wiggs

THE WORLD AS IT IS

IT'S a gay old world when you're gay,
And a glad old world when you're glad,
But whether you play
Or go toiling away,
It's a sad old world when you're sad.

It's a grand old world if you're great
And a mean old world if you're small;
It's a world full of hate
For the foolish who prate
Of the uselessness of it all.

It's a beautiful world to see,
Or it's dismal in every zone;
The thing it must be
In your gloom or your glee
Depends on yourself alone.

—S. E. Kiser

MY PHILOSOPHY

I ALLUS argy that a man
Who does about the best he can,
Is plenty good enough to suit
This lower mundane institute—
No matter ef his daily walk
Is subject fer his neighbor's talk,
And critic-minds of ev'ry whim
Jest all git up and go for him!

It's natchural enough, I guess,
When some gits more and some gits less,
For them-uns on the slimmest side
To claim it ain't a fair divide;
And I've knowed some to lay and wait,
And git up soon, and set up late,
To ketch some feller they could hate
Fer goin' at a faster gait.

The signs is bad when folks commence
A findin' fault with Providence,
And balkin' 'cause the earth don't shake
At every prancin' step they take.
No man is great till he can see
How less than little he would be
Ef stripped to self, and stark and bare
He hung his sign out anywhere.

My doctern is to lay aside
Contentions, and be satisfied:
Jest do your best, and praise er blame
That follers that, counts jest the same.
I've allus noticed grate success
Is mixed with troubles, more er less,
And it's the man who does the best
That gits more kicks than all the rest.

—James Whitcomb Riley

PRAYER AT MORNING

HE day returns and brings us the petty round of irritating concerns and duties. Help us to play the man, help us to perform them with laughter and kind faces, let cheerfulness abound with industry. Give us to go blithely on our business all this day, bring us to our resting beds weary and content and undishonored, and grant us in the end the gift of sleep.

—Robert Louis Stevenson

PRAYER AT EVENING

HE service of the day is over, and the hour come to rest. We resign into Thy hands our sleeping bodies, our cold hearths and open doors. Give us to awake with smiles, give us to labor smiling. As the sun returns in the east, so let our patience be renewed with dawn; as the sun lightens the world, so let our loving-kindness make bright this house of our habitations.

—Robert Louis Stevenson

FOUR things a man must learn to do
If he would make his record true:
To think without confusion clearly;
To love his fellow-men sincerely;
To act from honest motives purely;
To trust in God and heaven securely.

—Henry van Dyke

DO not forget that even as "to work is to worship," so to be cheery is to worship also; and to be happy is the first step to being pious.

—Robert Louis Stevenson

CHEERINESS is a thing to be more profoundly grateful for than all that genius ever inspired or talent ever accomplished. Next best to natural, spontaneous cheeriness, is deliberate, intended and persistent cheeriness, which we can create, can cultivate and can so foster and cherish that after a few years the world will never suspect that it was not an heredity gift.

—Helen Hunt Jackson

JOY does not happen. It is the inevitable result of certain lines followed and laws obeyed and so a matter of character

—Maltbie D. Babcock

I BELIEVE in gittin' as much good outen life as you kin—not that I ever set out to look fer happiness; seems like the folks that does, never finds it. I jes' do the best I kin where the good Lord put me at, an' it looks like I got a happy feelin' in me 'most all the time.

—Mrs. Wiggs

THAT happy state of mind, so rarely possessed, in which we can say, "I have enough," is the highest attainment of philosophy. Happiness consists, not in possessing much, but in being content with what we possess. He who wants little always has enough.

—Zimmerman

JUST BE GLAD

OH, HEART of mine, we shouldn't
    Worry so!
What we've missed of calm we couldn't
    Have, you know!
What we've met of stormy pain,
And of sorrow's driving rain,
We can better meet again
    If it blow.

For we know, not every morrow
    Can be sad;
So forgetting all the sorrow
    We have had,
Let us fold away our fears,
And put by our foolish tears,
And through all the coming years
    Just be glad.

—James Whitcomb Riley

GENIUS is talent set on fire by courage. Fidelity is simply daring to be true in small things as well as great. Courage is the standing army of the soul which keeps it from conquest, pillage and slavery.

—Henry van Dyke

GET into the habit of looking for the silver lining of the cloud, and when you have found it, continue to look at it rather than at the leaden gray in the middle. It will help you over many hated places.

—A. A. W.

FOUR-LEAF CLOVERS

I KNOW a place where the sun is like gold
And the cherry blooms burst forth with snow;
And down underneath is the loveliest nook,
Where the four-leaved clovers grow.

One leaf is for Hope, and one is for Faith,
And one is for Love, you know,
And God put another one in for Luck,—
If you search you will find where they grow.

But you must have Hope, and you must have Faith,
You must love and be strong, and so
If you work, if you wait, you will find the place,
Where the four-leaf clovers grow.

—Ella Higginson

THERE is only one way to be happy and that is to make somebody else so.

—Sidney Smith

IT IS the great boon of such characters as Mr. Lincoln's that they re-unite what God has joined together and man has put asunder. In him was vindicated the greatness of real goodness, and the goodness of real greatness.

—Philips Brooks

GET out and do something—work, sweat, hike, hump yourself—starve if need be—but dig on and deliver. Then talk if you want to, but the chances are you won't feel so much like it.

—James Howard Kehler

GRUMBLE? No, what's the good?
If it availed, I would;
But it doesn't a bit,
Not it.

Laugh? Yes, why not?
'Tis better than crying, a lot;
We were made to be glad,
Not sad.

Sing? Why, yes to be sure;
We shall better endure
If the heart's full of song
All day long.

IN MEN whom men condemn as ill
I find so much of goodness still;
In men whom men pronounce divine
I find so much of sin and blot,
I hesitate to draw a line
Between the two, where God has not.

I AM sure it is a great mistake always to know enough to go in
when it rains. One may keep snug and dry by such knowledge,
but one misses a world of loveliness.

—Adeline Knapp

THE block of granite which was an obstacle in the pathway of the
weak, becomes a stepping stone in the pathway of the strong.

—Thomas Carlyle

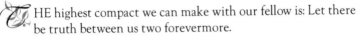

THE highest compact we can make with our fellow is: Let there be truth between us two forevermore.

—Ralph Waldo Emerson

STRAIGHT from the Mighty Bow this truth is driven: They fail, and they alone, who have not striven.

—Clarence Urmy

TO BELIEVE in the heroic makes heroes.

—Disraeli

LIFE without Industry is guilt. Industry without Art is brutality.

—John Ruskin

FOR a man to have an ideal in this world, for a man to know what an ideal is, this also is to have lived.

—Gerald Stanley Lee

PRAISE loudly; blame softly.

—Catherine II

THIS is the best day the world has ever seen. Tomorrow will be better.

—R. A. Campbell

THE ornaments of a house are the friends that frequent it.

—Ralph Waldo Emerson

THERE is ever a song somewhere, my dear,
Be the skies above or dark or fair,
There is ever a song that our hearts may hear—
There is ever a song somewhere, my dear—
There is ever a song somewhere!

—James Whitcomb Riley

THE reward is *in* keeping the commandments, not *for* keeping them.

—Lydia Marie Child

WHEN you play, play hard; when you work, don't play at all.

—Theodore Roosevelt

A WOMAN who creates and sustains a home, and under whose hands children grow up to be strong and pure men and women, is a creator second only to God.

—Helen Hunt Jackson

THIS is the beginning of all gospels, that the kingdom of Heaven is at hand just where we are.

WHETHER the world is blue or rosy depends upon the kind of spectacles we wear. It's our glasses, not the world, that needs attention.

NOAH was six hundred years old before he knew how to build an ark—don't lose your grip.

—Elbert Hubbard

CONCERN yourself but with Today;
Woo it, and teach it to obey
Your will and wish. Since time began
Today has been the friend of man,
But in his blindness and his sorrow
He looks to Yesterday and Tomorrow.

HAPPINESS is the only good. The place to be happy is here. The time to be happy is now. The way to be happy is to help make others so.

—Robert G. Ingersoll

MANY people are so afraid to die that they have never begun to live. But courage emancipates us and gives us to ourselves, that we may give ourselves freely and without fear to god.

—Henry van Dyke

EVERY mason in the quarry, every builder on the shore,
Every chopper in the palm grove, every raftsman at the oar—
Hewing wood and drawing water, splitting stones
        and cleaving sod —
All the dusty ranks of labor, in the regiments of God,
March together toward His triumph, do the task
        His hands prepare;
Honest toil is holy service; faithful work is praise and prayer.

—Henry van Dyke

WHEN things first got to goin' wrong with me, I says: "O Lord, whatever comes, keep me from gittin' sour!" Since then I've made it a practice to put all my worries down in the bottom of my heart, then set on the lid en' smile.

—Mrs. Wiggs

I HEARD a raven croak, but I persuaded myself it was the song of the nightingale. I smelled the smell of the mould, but thought of the violets it nourished.

—Tom Hood

YOU have not fulfilled every duty unless you have fulfilled that of being pleasant.

—Charles Buxton

THE grand essentials of happiness are something to do, something to love, and something to hope for.

—Chalmers

NOTHING is so contagious as enthusiasm. It is the real allegory of the tale of Orpheus. It moves stones, it charms brutes. Enthusiasm is the genius of sincerity and truth accomplishes no victories without it.

—Bulwer

HE WHO goes down into the battle of life giving a smile for every frown, a cheery word for every cross one, and lending a helping hand to the unfortunate is, after all, the best of missionaries.

PASS IT ON

HAVE you had a kindness shown?
    Pass it on!
'Twas not given to you alone!
    Pass it on!
Let it travel down the years,
Let it wipe another's tears,
Till in Heaven the deed appears;
    Pass it on!

—Henry Burton

"WHAT helped you over the great obstacles of life?" was asked a successful man. "The other obstacles," he replied.

WHAT we see depends mainly on what we look for.

—John Lubbock

THEY can, because they believe they can.

—Virgil

TO love and win is the best thing;
To love and lose the next best.

—W. M. Thackeray

SOME defeats are only instalments of victory.

—Jacob A. Riis

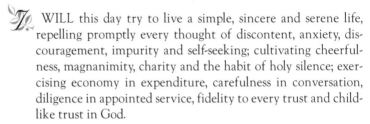

I. WILL this day try to live a simple, sincere and serene life, repelling promptly every thought of discontent, anxiety, discouragement, impurity and self-seeking; cultivating cheerfulness, magnanimity, charity and the habit of holy silence; exercising economy in expenditure, carefulness in conversation, diligence in appointed service, fidelity to every trust and childlike trust in God.

—John H. Vincent

B. ELIEVE in the better side of men. It is optimism that really saves people.

—Ian Maclaren

I. SHALL pass through this world but once. Any good thing that I can do, or any kindness I can show to any human being, let me do it now—for I shall not pass this way again.

T. O ENTER Heaven a man must take it with him.

—Henry Drummond

T. HE Kingdom of Heaven is not a place, but a state of mind.

—John Burroughs

I. DO the best I know. The very best I can; and I mean to keep right on doing so until the end. If the end brings me out all right, what is said against me won't amount to anything. If the end brings me out wrong, ten angels swearing I was right would make no difference.

—Abraham Lincoln

A PRAYER

NOT more of light, I ask, O God,
But eyes to see what is;
Not sweeter songs, but power to hear
The present melodies.

Not greater strength, but how to use
The power that I possess;
Not more of love, but skill to turn
A frown to a caress.

Not more of joy, but power to feel
Its kindling presence near;
To give to others all I have
Of courage and of cheer.

Give me all fears to dominate,
All holy joys to know;
To be the friend I wish to be,
To speak the truth I know.

—Florence Holbrook

ANY one can carry his burden, however heavy, till nightfall. Any one can do his work, however hard, for one day. Any one can live sweetly, lovingly, purely, till the sun goes down. And this is all that life really means.

THE world is looking for the man who can do something, not for the man who can "explain" why he didn't do it.

TRUE bravery is shown by performing without witnesses what one might be capable of doing before all the world.

—La Rochefoucauld

THE best preacher is the heart; the best teacher is time; the best book is the world; the best friend is God.

—The *Talmud*

'TIS not the weight of jewel or plate,
    Or the fondle of silk or fur;
'Tis the spirit in which the gift is rich,
    As the gifts of the wise ones were;
And we are not told whose gift was gold,
    Or whose was the gift of myrrh.

THE Indian says that when a man kills a foe the strength of the slain enemy passes into the victor's arm. In the weird fancy lies the truth. Each defeat leaves us weaker for the next battle, but each conquest makes us stronger. Nothing makes a prison to a human life, but a defeated, broken spirit. The bird in its cage that sings all the while is not a captive.

—J. R. Miller

BELIEVE in yourself, believe in humanity, believe in the success of your undertakings. Fear nothing and no one. Love your work. Work, hope, trust. Keep in touch with today. Teach yourself to be practical and up-to-date and sensible. You cannot fail!

*G*ENIUS seems to be allied to immortal youth. Goethe at eighty-four had the same deep interest in life that he felt at thirty or forty; and Gladstone at eighty-six was one of the most eager and aspiring men of his time.

—Hamilton Wright Mabie

A CERTAIN amount of opposition is a great help to a man; kites rise against and not with the wind.

*B*LESSED is he who has found his work; let him ask no other blessedness. He has a work, a life purpose; he has found it, and will follow it!

—Thomas Carlyle

*K*ING HASSAN, well-beloved, was wont to say,
When aught went wrong, or any labor failed,
"Tomorrow, friends, will be another day!"
And in that faith he slept, and so prevailed.

*A*H! LET us fill our hearts up with the glory of the day,
And banish ev'ry doubt and care and sorrow far away!
For the world is full of roses, and the roses full of dew,
And the dew is full of heavenly love that drips for me and you.

—James Whitcomb Riley

*M*AKE the most of yourself, for that is all there is of you.

—Ralph Waldo Emerson

COMPENSATION

THE universe pays every man in his own coin; if you smile, it smiles upon you in return; if you frown, you will be frowned at; if you sing, you will be invited into gay company; if you think, you will be entertained by thinkers; and if you love the world and earnestly seek for the good that is therein, you will be surrounded by loving friends, and nature will pour into your lap the treasures of the earth. Censure, criticise and hate, and you will be censured, criticised and hated by your fellow men. Every seed brings forth after its kind. Mistrust begets mistrust, and confidence begets confidence, kindness begets kindness, love begets love. Resist and you will be resisted. To meet the aggressive assault every entity rises up rigid and impenetrable— while yonder mountain of granite melts and floats away on the bosom of the river of love.

—N. W. Zimmerman

LIVING will teach you how to live, better than preacher or book.

—Goethe

THE unhappy are always wrong; wrong in being so, wrong in saying so, wrong in needing help of others.

WRITE on your hearts that every day is the best day of the year.

—Ralph Waldo Emerson

HE WHO has conferred a kindness should be silent; he who has received one should speak of it.

—Seneca

NOT one holy day, but seven.
Worshipping not at the call of a bell,
But at the call of my soul.
    Singing not at the baton's sway,
But to the rhythm in my heart.
Loving because I must.
Giving because I cannot keep.
Doing for the joy of it.

—Muriel Strode

IF I can stop one heart from breaking,
    I shall not live in vain.
If I can ease one life the aching,
    Or cool one pain,
Or help one fainting Robin
    Into his nest again
    I shall not live in vain.

—Emily Dickinson

CHEERFULNESS and content are great beautifiers and are famous preservers of youthful looks.

—Charles Dickens

"WHATEVER the weather may be," says he,
"Whatever the weather may be,
It's the songs ye sing, an' the smiles ye wear,
That's a-makin' the sun shine everywhere."

—James Whitcomb Riley

UP, MY HEART, AND SING

THE dark, dark night is gone,
The lark is on the wing,
From bleak and barren fields he soars,
Eternal hope to sing.

And shall I be less brave
Than yon sweet lyric thing?
From deeps of failure and despair,
Up, up my heart, and sing!

The dark, dark year is gone:
The red blood of the spring
Will quicken Nature's pulses soon,
So up, my heart, and sing!

—Ella Higginson

THIS is the gospel of labor,
Ring it, ye bells of the kirk,
The Lord of Love came down from above,
To live with the men who work.
This is the rose He planted,
Here in the thorn-cursed soil;
Heaven is blessed with perfect rest,
But the blessing of earth is toil.

—Henry van Dyke

I DO not know of any way so sure of making others
happy as being so one's self.

—Sir Arthur Helps

LET me but do my work day to day
In field or forest, at this desk or loom,
In roaring market place or tranquil room;
Let me but find it in my heart to say,
When vagrant wishes beckon me astray,
"This is my work; my blessing, not my doom,
Of all who live, I am the one by whom
This work can best be done in the right way."

Then shall I see it not too great, nor small
To suit my spirit and to prove my powers;
Then shall I, cheerful, greet the laboring hours,
And cheerful turn, when the long shadows fall
At eventide, to play and love and rest
Because I know for me my work is best.

—Henry van Dyke

MAKE the best of everything;
Think the best of everybody;
Hope the best for yourself.

—George Stephenson

TO BE serene amid a losing fight,
To meet with equal courage dark or light,
To hate all sham, and with persistent might
To do brave deeds as in a master's sight,—
This is to learn life's lesson, reach the height.

—Charles Allen Dausson

IF you strike a thorn or rose,
　　Keep a-goin'.
If it hails or if it snows,
　　Keep-a-goin'.
'Tain't no use to sit and whine
When the fish ain't on your line;
Bait your hook and keep on tryin'—
　　Keep a-goin'.
When the weather kills your crop,
　　Keep a-goin'.
When you tumble from the top,
　　Keep a-goin'.
S'pose you're out o' every dime!
Gettin' broke ain't any crime;
Tell the world you're feeling prime—
　　Keep a-goin'.
When it looks like all is up,
　　Keep a-goin'.
Drain the sweetness from the cup,
　　Keep a-goin'.
See the wild bird on the wing,
Hear the bells that sweetly ring,
When you feel like sighin', sing.
　　Keep a-goin'.

　　　　　　　　　　—Frank L. Stanton

TAKE Joy home,
And make a place in thy great heart for her;
Then will she come, and oft will sing to thee,
When thou art working in the furrows; aye,
Or weeding in the sacred hour of dawn.
It is a comely fashion to be glad—
Joy is the grace we say to God.

—Jean Ingelow

THE little cares that fretted me,
I lost them yesterday,
Among the fields above the sea,
Among the winds at play;
Among the lowing of the herds,
The rustling of the trees,
Among the singing of the birds,
The humming of the bees.
The foolish fears of what may happen,
I cast them all away,
Among the clover-scented grass,
Among the new-mown hay,
Among the husking of the corn
Where drowsy poppies nod,
Where ill thoughts die and good are born,
Out in the fields with God.

—E. B. Browning

SHAKE!

IT'S great to say "Good Morning,"
  It's fine to say "Hello,"
But better still to grasp the hand
  Of a loyal friend you know.

A look may be forgotten,
  A word misunderstood,
But the touch of the human hand
  Is the pledge of brotherhood.

—E. O. G.

WHAT do we live for if not to make the world less difficult for each other?

—George Eliot

TOMORROW you have no business with. You steal if you touch tomorrow. It is God's. Every day has in it enough to keep any man occupied without concerning himself with the things beyond.

—Henry Ward Beecher

TAKE what is; trust what may be; that's life's true lesson.

—Robert Browning

IF we were charged so much a head for sunsets, or if God sent round a drum before the hawthornes come into flower, what a work we should make about their beauty!

—Robert Louis Stevenson

LISTEN to the Exhortation of the Dawn.
    Look to the Day,
For it is Life, the very life of Life.
In its brief course lie all the Verities
And Realities of your Existence,
The bliss of Truth, the glory of Action,
    The splendor of Beauty,
For Yesterday is but a dream
And Tomorrow is only a vision,
    But Today,
Well lived, makes every Yesterday
    A dream of happiness
And every Tomorrow a vision of Hope.
    Look well, therefore, to the Day.
Such is the Salutation of the Dawn.

—from the Sanskrit

MAKE one person happy each day and in forty years you have made 14,600 human beings happy for a little time at least.

IF I cannot do great things, I can do small things in a great way.

—James Freeman Clarke

DESIRE joy and thank God for it. Renounce it, if need be, for other's sake. That's joy beyond joy.

—Robert Browning

DEAR Lord, kind Lord,
Gracious Lord! I pray
Thou wilt look on all I love
    Tenderly today.
Weed their hearts of weariness;
    Scatter every care,
Down a wake of angel wings
    Winnowing the air.

Bring unto the sorrowing
    All release from pain;
Let the lips of laughter
    Overflow again!
And with all the needy,
    Oh! divide, I pray,
This vast treasure of content
    That is mine today.

—James Whitcomb Riley

GOODNESS does not more certainly make men happy, than happiness makes them good.

—Walter Savage Landor

IN months of sun so live that in months of rain thou shalt still be happy.

—from the "Mahabharata"

*H*OWEVER the battle is ended,
    Though proudly the victor comes
With fluttering flags and prancing nags
    And echoing roll of drums,
Still Truth proclaims this motto
    In letters of living light—
No question is ever settled
    Until it is settled right.

Let those who have failed take courage,
    Though the enemy seemed to have won,
Though his rank be strong, if he be in the wrong,
    The battle is not yet done.
For sure as the morning follows
    The darkest hour of night,
No question is ever settled
    Until it is settled right.

O man bowed down with labor,
    O woman young, yet old;
O heart oppressed in the toiler's breast,
    And crushed by the power of gold,
Keep on with your weary battle
    Against triumphant night;
No question is ever settled
    Until it is settled right.

                        —Ella Wheeler Wilcox

*E*VERY man is an optimist who sees deep enough.

                        —Edwin Atkinson

SMILE a little,
Help a little,
Push a little,
    The world needs you.
Work a little,
Wait a little,
Hope a little,
    And don't get blue.

—E. O. G.

THEY might not need me—yet they might,
I'll let my heart be just in sight.
A smile so small as mine might be
Precisely their necessity.

—Emily Dickinson

FIGHT when you are down; die hard—determine at least to do—
and you won't die at all.

—James H. West

NO one has any more right to go about unhappy than he has to
go about ill-bred. He owes it to himself, to his friends, to society, and to the community in general, to live up to his best spiritual possibilities, not only now and then, once or twice a year,
or once in a season, but every day and every hour.

—Lilian Whiting

THE DEEPEST WORTH

THESE are the things I prize
And hold of deepest worth:
  Light of the sapphire skies,
  Peace of the silent hills,
Shelter of forest, comfort of the grass,
Shadow of clouds that swiftly pass,
    And after showers
    The smell of flowers,
      And of the good brown earth,—
    And best of all, along the way,
      Friendship and mirth.

                              —Henry van Dyke

IT IS GOOD TO BE ALIVE

T is good to be alive when the trees shine green,
    And the steep red hills stand up against the sky;
Big sky, blue sky, with flying clouds between—
    It is good to be alive and see the clouds drive by!

It is good to be alive when the strong winds blow,
    The strong, sweet winds blowing straightly off the sea;
Great sea, green sea, with swinging ebb and flow—
    It is good to be alive and see the waves run by.

                              —Charlotte Perkins Stetson

GOD has given us tongues that we may say something pleasant to
our fellow-men.

                              —Heinrich Heine

SUCCESS

*H*E HAS achieved success who has lived well, laughed often, and loved much; who has gained the respect of intelligent men, and the love of little children; who has filled his niche and accomplished his task; who has left the world better than he found it, whether by an improved poppy, a perfect poem, or a rescued soul; who has never lacked appreciation of earth's beauty, or failed to express it; who has always looked for the best in others and given the best he had; whose life was an inspiration; whose memory a benediction.

—Bessie A. Stanley

*I*T is an everlasting duty—the duty of being brave.

—Thomas Carlyle

RESOLVE

*T*O keep my health!
To do my work!
To live!
To see to it I grow and gain and give!
Never to look behind me for an hour!
To wait in weakness, and to walk in power;
But always fronting onward toward the light,
Always and always facing toward the right.
Robbed, starved, defeated, fallen, wide astray—
On, with what strength I have!
Back to the way!

—Charlotte Perkins Stetson

KEEP A PULLIN'

*F*ISH don't bite just for the wishin',
      Keep a pullin'!
Change your bait and keep on fishin';
      Keep a pullin'!
Luck ain't nailed to any spot;
Men you envy, like as not,
Envy you your job and lot!
      Keep a pullin'!

ALWAYS WITH YOU

*S*AY not "Welcome" when I come,
      Nor "Farewell" tell me when I go;
For I come not when I come,
      And I go not when I go.

I am always, *ever* with you,
      Always will be, so I pray.
I would never "Welcome" give you
      And "Farewell" would never say.

*E*VERY man should keep a fair-sized cemetery in which to bury the faults of his friends.

—Henry Ward Beecher

*N*EVER attempt to bear more than one kind of trouble at once. Some people bear three kinds—all they have had, all they have now, and all they expect to have

—Edward Everett Hale

*T*HE world is wide
In time and tide,
And God is guide;
    Then do not hurry.
That man is blest
Who does his best
And leaves the rest;
    Then do not worry.

—C. F. Deems

A RESOLVE

*T*O stand by one's friend to the uttermost end,
    And fight a fair fight with one's foe;
Never to quit and never to twit,
    And never to peddle one's woe.

—George Brinton Chandler

*O*PPORTUNITIES correspond with almost mathematical accuracy, to the ability to use them.

—Lilian Whiting

*T*HERE is no defeat except from within. There is really no insurmountable barrier save your own inherent weakness of purpose.

—Ralph Waldo Emerson

*N*O man imparteth his joy to his friend, but he joyeth the more; and no man imparteth his grief to his friend, but he grieveth the less.

—Lord Bacon

*H*APPINESS, at least, is not solitary; it joys to communicate; it loves others, for it depends on them for its existence; it sanctions and encourages to all delights that are not unkind in themselves. The very name and appearance of a happy man breathe of good-nature, and help the rest of us to live.

—Robert Louis Stevenson

*J*ES go 'long good natured,
 Dat's de safes' way;
Sun goes on a-beamin'
 An' a-smilin' all de day.
Keeps de crops a-growin'
 An' de blossoms, an' de fruits,
Until de storm come 'round an' try
 To lif' 'em by the roots.

Sun goes on a-shinin'
 Up above de cloud;
Wind it keeps a-blowin'
 And de thunder rattles loud;
Sky gits blue an' peaceful,
 Like no storm ain' never bin—
Sun he stays good-natured
 An' he allus boun' to win.

*A*N AIM in life is the only fortune worth the finding; and it is not to be found in foreign lands, but in the heart itself.

—Robert Louis Stevenson

A HAPPY THOUGHT

THE world is so full of a number of things,
I'm sure we should all be as happy as kings.

—Robert Louis Stevenson

THIS world's no blot for us, nor blank; it means intensely, and means good.

—Robert Browning

WOULD you throw away a diamond because it pricked you? One good friend is not to be weighed against the jewels of all the earth. If there is coolness or unkindness between us, let us come face to face and have it out. Quick, before love grows cold!

—Robert Smith

THE years monotonous? The same old seasons, and weathers, and aspects of nature? Never anything new to admire or wonder at? The monotony is in our eyesight, which goes on seeing nothing but the common and invariable things; simply because, from long familiarity, these are the easy things to see. But these are only the frame of the picture; the picture is never twice alike.

—Edward Rowland Sill

NOT what you do, but how you do it, is the test of your capacity.

A LAUGH is worth a hundred groans in any market.

—Charles Lamb

ONE makes one's own happiness only by taking care of the happiness of others.

—Saint-Pierre

SMILE

SMILE!
The world is blue enough
Without your feeling blue.

Smile!
There's not half joy enough
Unless you're happy too.

Smile!
The sun is always shining,
And there's work to do.

Smile!
This world may not be Heaven,
But then it's Home to you.

—E. O. G.

IN his own life, then, a man is not to expect happiness, only to profit by it gladly when it shall arise. Somehow or other, though he does not know what goodness is, he must try to be good; somehow or other, though he cannot tell what will do it, he must try to give happiness to others.

—Robert Louis Stevenson

THE BOOK OF GOOD CHEER

*Y*ES, they whose feet upon good errands run
Are friends of God, with Michael of the sun;
Yes, each accomplished service of the day
Paves for the feet of God a lordlier way.
The souls that love and labor through all wrong,
They clasp His hand and make the circle strong:
They lay the deep foundations, stone by stone,
And build into Eternity God's throne.

—Edwin Markham

*T*IME is infinitely long, and each day is a vessel into which a great deal may be poured—if one will actually fill it up.

—Goethe

*P*OWER dwells with cheerfulness.

—Ralph Waldo Emerson

*I*F I have done aught for you, oh friend, I do not ask that you return the favor, but do for God's sake pass it on.

—James Howard Kehler

*I*N THE morning when thou risest unwillingly, let this thought be present—"I am rising to the work of a human being."

—Marcus Aurelius

*A*N ASPIRATION is joy forever, a possession as solid as a landed estate.

—Robert Louis Stevenson

PEOPLE who lead busy lives never find time to have hysterics.

—J. M. Studley

THE best rose-bush, after all, is not that which has the fewest thorns, but that which bears the finest roses.

—Henry van Dyke

NOT how much talent have I, but how much will to use the talent that I have, is the main question.

—W. C. Gannett

A HAPPY man or woman is a better thing to find than a five-pound note—they practically demonstrate the Theorem of the Livableness of Life.

—Robert Louis Stevenson

BE PLEASANT until ten o'clock in the morning, and the rest of the day will take care of itself.

I FIND the gayest castles in the air that were ever piled far better for comfort and for use than the dungeons in the air that are daily dug and caverned out by grumbling, discontented people. A man should make life and nature happier to us, or he had better never been born.

—Ralph Waldo Emerson

IF I were you I would not worry. Just make up your mind to do better when you get another chance, and be content with that.

—Beatrice Harraden

THE year's at the spring,
And the day's at the morn;
Morning's at seven;
The hillside's dew-pearled;
The lark's on the wing;
The snail's on the thorn;
God's in His heaven—
All's right with the world!

—Robert Browning

WE HAVE only to trust and do our best, and wear a smiling face, as may be, for ourselves and others.

—Robert Louis Stevenson

THE perfect model makes the perfect copy. The successful finish of everything on earth depends on the right thought which brought it into being.

—Agnes Greene Foster

THERE are persons so radiant, so genial, so kind, so pleasure-bearing, that you instinctively feel in their presence that they do you good, whose coming into a room is like the bringing of a lamp there.

—Henry Ward Beecher

IF there is any person to whom you feel a dislike, that is the person of whom you ought never to speak.

—Richard Cecil

INVICTUS

*O*UT of the night that covers me,
    Black as the Pit from pole to pole,
I thank whatever gods may be
    For my unconquerable soul.

In the fell clutch of circumstance
    I have not winced nor cried aloud.
Under the bludgeoning of chance
    My head is bloody, but unbowed.

Beyond this place of wrath and tears
    Looms but the horror of the shade,
And yet the menace of the years
    Finds and shall find me, unafraid.

It matters not how strait the gate,
    How charged with punishment the scroll,
I am the master of my fate;
    I am the captain of my soul.
                                            —William Ernest Henley

*T*O SIT still and contemplate—to remember the faces of women without desire, to be pleased with the great deeds of men without envy, to be everything and everywhere in sympathy, and yet content to remain where and what you are—is not this to know both wisdom and virtue, and to dwell with happiness?
                                            —Robert Louis Stevenson

L'ENVOI

WHEN earth's last picture is painted, and the tubes
    are twisted and dried,
When the oldest colors have faded, and the youngest
    critic has died.
We shall rest, and, faith, we shall need it—lie down for
    an aeon or two.
Till the Master of All Good Workmen shall set us to
    work anew!

And those that were good will be happy: they shall sit
    in a golden chair;
They shall splash at a ten-league canvas with brushes
    of comet's hair;
They shall find real saints to draw from—Magdalene,
    Peter and Paul;
They shall work for an age at a sitting and never be
    tired at all;

And only the Master shall praise us, and only the
    Master shall blame;
And no one shall work for money, and no one shall
    work for fame;
But each for the joy of the working, and each, in his
    separate star,
Shall draw the Thing as he sees It for the God of
    Things as They Are!

—Rudyard Kipling